Not About Birds

Glen C. Griffin, M.D.
Mary Ella Griffin, R.N.

Illustrated by Heidi Darley

Deseret Book Company
Salt Lake City, Utah
1979

Library of Congress Cataloging in Publication Data

Griffin, Glen C
   Not about birds.

   SUMMARY: Presents basic information about reproduc-
tion and discusses masturbation, birth control, marriage,
and relationships with parents and friends from a Mormon
point of view.
    1. Sex instruction for youth.   [1. Sex instruction
for youth.   2. Sexual ethics]   I. Griffin, Mary Ella,
1936-   joint author.   II. Title.
HQ35.G75   301.41′07   79-16653
ISBN 0-87747-753-1

Especially for
Janell and Bob,
Joan, Mark, Gary,
Jill, and Greg . . .
and all their friends, everywhere

Contents

Preface

illions of books, tapes, computers, and brains are crammed with information. Our problem is to sort out the correct from the questionable from the totally wrong. The funny baldheaded king in *The King and I* explained this difficulty as he sang, "In my head are many facts of which I wish I was more certain I was sure." Then he concluded that "experts" are not always right.

For example, for a long time biologists thought there were forty-eight chromosomes in a normal human cell. Now the experts think there are forty-six. The king, thinking over his wisdom, put it this way: "There are times I almost think I am not sure of what I absolutely know!"

The search for answers is not easy. But eternal truths will always be true, and they can help us find happiness that will last forever.

Girls

Girls! Could anything be more interesting? A girl's curves attract much attention. But these curves are more than decoration.

Amazing things happen within the gentle curves of the breasts—miracles that are difficult to imagine. Whenever needed, hundreds of things automatically happen. The result is a smooth, almost white liquid. Various proteins, fat, lactose, minerals, and water turn into milk, which is nutritionally perfect. Within each breast are some eighteen separate milk-producing glands, which are protected and insulated by well-placed fat cells. Each of the eighteen-or-so milk glands has its own duct that carries its milk to the nipple.

The mammary glands are so small in infants and young girls that they are almost not noticeable. Then at about age ten or eleven, a gland on one side may get a slight headstart, developing just enough to cause a little, tender bump. Usually nothing else happens for a while, until at puberty both breasts increase in size rather suddenly. Variations in development and timing become big worries to most girls, because breast development seems to announce that a girl is becoming a woman. But there is no relationship between breast size and femininity, or ability to provide perfect nourishment for a baby. Almost every mother, no matter her size, can have more than enough milk for her babies. And what a joy nursing a baby is, to say nothing of the benefits that a baby receives from a mother's milk.

Femininity? Yes, the breasts are a symbol of femininity, but in a much more important way than many people think. Femininity is more than just looks or appearance. That's only part of it. Femininity also includes the possibility of being a wife and mother.

And there is more that is amazing about the female body—particularly the ovaries, fallopian tubes, uterus, and vagina. A girl has two ovaries and two fallopian tubes. Why two? As with many paired body parts, the two function well together, but each is capable of carrying on should anything ever happen to the other.

Each ovary is about the size of an almond, with one located on each side in the lower part of the body. At birth the ovaries already contain more than a lifetime supply of eggs, maybe as many as half a million! Of these, only four or five hundred will ever become mature and ready to be fertilized. And of these, very few ever actually become fertilized.

Suddenly, as a girl approaches puberty, the ovaries begin to produce some hormones that change a girl into a woman. This may happen at age twelve or eleven, thirteen or fifteen, or even later. It doesn't really matter when it happens, because it is much earlier than necessary for a girl to become a wife and mother. However, waiting for the changes to occur sometimes causes a girl some anxious moments, maybe even months and years.

When the ovaries start producing the estrogen hormone, all sorts of things begin to happen. The glands and other structures in the breasts develop, the pelvis widens, and body hair begins to appear, as do some soft pads of fat that help shape the breasts and hips.

About this time the pituitary gland, located in the head, begins monthly cycles of releasing a tiny dose of a powerful substance called follicle-stimulating hormone, or FSH. This substance somehow brings to life a few egg cells in the ovary, which begin to move to the surface of the ovary in bubbles or follicles. One of these fluid-filled bubbles, which is now larger than a pea, waits on the surface of the ovary for lutenizing hormone to cause the bubble to explode. When this happens, the mature egg is allowed to fall into the funnel-like opening of the fallopian tube.

From the ovary on each side, a fallopian tube leads to, and opens into, the uterus. The egg, or ovum, moves through the fallopian tube and travels to the uterus. On the way, if sperm are present, the egg might become fertilized.

The uterus is an upside-down, hollow, pear-shaped organ located in the middle of the pelvis. It is made up of a complicated arrangement of muscle fibers with a soft lining. The uterus has three openings: two at the top from the fallopian tubes and a larger opening at the bottom—the cervix. The cervix opens into the vagina. This is also where the male sperm enter, and the passage through which the baby leaves the uterus and the mother.

Another amazing thing happens when the follicle pops, freeing the egg from the ovary. When the follicle bursts, a crater is left on the ovary. This crater fills in with some special new cells that produce another hormone, called progesterone. Progesterone stimulates the inside of the uterus to make a thick, soft lining, rich in blood. This special lining is a perfect new home for a fertilized egg. If there is no fertilized egg, all the special lining tissues and the blood in them are discarded by the body, through a process called menstruation.

The menstrual flow that leaves the cervix and vagina usually lasts from three to five days. The timing is intricate. It's all part of a complex cycle. Often for the first few years, this timing is quite irregular. Why it works so well most of the time is a miracle, and why the timing sometimes misses a little is no wonder at all.

There are endless questions we could ask about the amazing female. How is it that each month usually just one ovum is discharged from one or the other ovary? How does the pear-shaped uterus expand sufficiently to contain a growing baby? How does a sac form with fluid to protect the growing baby? Why do some cells form a placenta and umbilical cord to nourish the baby? How does the uterus know when to contract as the time approaches for the baby to be born? And how can the cervix open wide enough to allow a baby to slip through into the vagina? The fantastic human body and its reproductive system are not happenstance. Some of our questions can be answered and some cannot.

One thing is certain—a girl's body is precious. Becoming pregnant and giving birth to a baby is an amazing sequence of events. This ability includes strong feelings and desires. Such feelings are good. The desires to use these creative abilities are normal and to be expected. But there are right and wrong times and circumstances when these abilities should be used. This may seem very obvious, but what about desires occurring at inappropriate times? Some people don't bother about controlling them. They just let desires and urges set into motion actions that involve sacred parts of the body. But a girl with eternal goals wants to remain in control, and to avoid inappropriate desires and actions. A girl who is in control does not allow herself or anyone else, male or female, to touch or excite her body in such a way that these powerful desires progress.

Control is important because these feelings may become so strong that they overpower beliefs. Unchecked, they may lead to problems. So the ability to control and use these desires and powers wisely makes a big difference during life and in eternity. All these things affect how a girl may feel or think or act at any particular time. Thinking one thing and feeling another can be a problem. It's confusing when our mind tells us one thing and our emotions tell us another.

And then there's the matter of menstrual periods and schedules. Periods, along with tampons or pads, are somewhat inconvenient. Sometimes there is some discomfort. Girls usually try to be discreet at such times, acting as though nothing is happening. Often their efforts are so effective that no one knows. At other times it's not so easy. Boys usually don't really understand all about these problems, and it's easy to misjudge a girl at one of these times.

When it comes to other people, girls seem to have special capacities to understand about feelings, hurts, and problems. There is something about girls and mothers that makes them compassionate and helpful. Thank goodness for mothers and girls who care about others, wanting everything to come out all right.

But there are times when a girl may feel threatened by other girls. Sometimes girls can be very cruel to each other. A girl may feel totally rejected by a group. Even popular girls on some days feel as if they have been pushed out of a group. This is why most girls develop a special friendship with one other girl. These two often become very dependent on each other. They may do everything together to such an extent that one may seem the shadow of the other. Sometimes these friendships last for a lifetime, and sometimes they don't. Especially when girls start getting interested in boys, it can be difficult for one girl to stand by and see her special friend go places and do things with a boy. She may feel left out of the new boy-girl relationship. Sometimes such problems occur even in the courting years. With maturity, girls can handle both girl friends and boy friends and the many interactions and competitions, but all through these years there are ups and downs. Looking ahead to having a forever partner and companion is a great goal. This objective can help smooth out some difficult times along the way.

Everyone needs recognition—to feel important and needed. Every girl is important, and is needed, even though at some moments it may not seem so. When we consider the whole of our existence, including our preexistence along with celestial eternity, everything about life becomes more meaningful. For some who never see this perspective or others who forget about it, values may easily become mixed up.

Just as a girl is born with ovaries containing a lifetime supply of ova, so is she born with the priceless possessions of purity and virginity. What she does with these possessions means everything, in earth life and in eternity. A girl has forever ahead of her, and many important things to do along the way. Every day is a great adventure even when it doesn't seem like much is happening. It is. Today is a very important day and so is tomorrow. Marriage and motherhood are exciting experiences to come, at the right time and with the right companion. Being a girl is wonderful. And being a boy who can fall in love with a girl can be just as special.

Boys

Five hundred million sperm may be released at a time. Five hundred million! Sperm, of course, are produced in the testicles, but only after a boy physically matures. Then sperm are produced by the multimillions.

The testicles, sometimes called the testes, are the main reproductive organs of the male. There are two of them, about the size of pecans. They are located between the thighs in a sac called the scrotum.

The testicles are so sensitive that the slightest injury to them can cause extreme pain. This is rather common in rough competitive sports, such as football and soccer. After a jolt or injury, the pain is so intense that a player often can't get up for several minutes. Why are they so tender? One reason is so they will be protected carefully—and they usually are.

Testicles are also particularly sensitive to temperature—the normal body temperature is too warm for them! That is why the testicles are in the loose sac of skin called

the scrotum, rather than being located inside the body.

The testicles need to be at a constant temperature that is three degrees below the rest of the body's normal temperature. When the environment is cold, the scrotal sac pulls the testicles up closer to the body so they won't get too cold. When the body is hot, the sac becomes loose. This accomplishes two things: the testicles are farther away from the too warm body, and the scrotum itself gets rid of excess heat through an evaporative cooling process.

These amazing testicles produce testosterone, the hormone that changes a boy into a man. Because of testosterone, whiskers grow, body hair appears, the voice deepens, and other body characteristics develop that are typical of manliness.

But of all the astonishing things about the male reproductive system, the most interesting are the sperm, those wiggly creatures with tails. A sperm is the smallest cell in the male body, while an ovum is the largest cell in the female body.

After sperm are produced in the testes, they travel in a special fluid through spermatic ducts to the prostate gland and into the urethra, which is the pathway through the penis to the outside. The penis, of course, is the male external reproductive organ, and is covered by loose skin. Sometimes the skin at the end is removed in an operation called a circumcision. There are differences of opinion about whether it is a good idea to always do this. The main advantage is that after circumcision, keeping the area clean is somewhat easier. Otherwise, everything works just the same in a male who has been circumcised as in one who has not had the surgery. If circumcision is to be done, it is usually done soon after birth.

Another interesting thing about the male body is the structural engineering of the male reproductive organ, the penis. The urethra is the passageway through it. This is the way the urine gets out of the body. It is also the route the sperm take. Some may wonder if having a common passageway for the urine and sperm is a problem. It isn't. The routing of these two functions is well controlled. Urine can enter the urethra and pass out of the body only when the penis is soft and limp. However, when sperm are to be released, blood fills a closed spongelike network in the penis, making it firm and erect. This firmness makes it possible for the penis to enter the female vagina. How does the system switch from one function to the other? Under some circumstances it is automatic, and under other circumstances there is conscious control. With such a complex system it is helpful to know what to expect, and how to avoid turning on the reproductive system at inappropriate times.

The procreative power is dynamic. It might be compared to nuclear energy, which, when used unwisely, can result in disaster. Control of one's reproductive power deserves the same careful control as does nuclear energy. When a boy's body reaches maturity, sperm are produced. These sperm are able to fertilize long before it is time for marriage and mating. During this time it is very important to control them.

Sperm don't just wait for years to pass and for marriage to take place so they can be useful. From the time a boy matures, countless sperm are alive and moving about in a special fluid, ready to leave the body. This process goes on for many years, slowly before there is a need, and more rapidly when there is a need. When mating does not occur—which, of course, it should not outside of marriage—the sperm and its seminal fluid are discharged from time to time during sleep, without any effort or control. Sometimes this is an inconvenience, just as menstrual

10

periods are inconvenient for girls. This process happens to every mature male who is not regularly mating, and should not be a source of worry or distress.

However, intentional self-stimulation is not acceptable. Self-stimulation, called masturbation, causes the spongy cavities to become full, which is called an erection, followed by the discharge of sperm. Even though masturbation is common, it is wrong. No matter what anyone may say, it is not possible to be in tune with one's heavenly parents while tampering with such a sacred process. Masturbation can become a terrible habit. It can become a vicious cycle. This habit can become as strong as smoking, and as difficult to control. Another problem with masturbation is that more serious moral transgressions may easily follow.

Masturbation is evidence of lack of control. The Lord, through his prophets, has said very positively that it is a sin. This should be sufficient. If this has been a problem, fathers and bishops are helpful sources of advice and assistance. If this has not been a problem, avoiding it entirely should be the goal of every boy.

The male reproductive organs are easily stimulated. Sometimes the slightest thought or glance or touch can send blood rushing into the spongelike spaces, causing an erection. This may occur at totally inappropriate moments—sometimes when there has been no intention to start the process. It might occur when a boy and girl are seemingly harmlessly near each other. This is why it is so important to avoid any situation where there is any possibility of things getting out of control. Most people in such a dangerous situation don't realize how quickly and how unintentionally the situation can get out of control. Once a chain of events begins, chastity may be easily lost. Anyone looking toward celestial marriage will want to avoid any circumstances that might lead to the loss of future blessings.

Because of the differences in body responses, a girl may feel very much in control of herself when she is very close to a boy who is rapidly losing control. Avoiding such circumstances is just as important as avoiding leaning too far over a cliff to get a better view. If control ever seems to be slipping, waiting even a few moments to get out of the circumstances may result in disaster as well as embarrassment. Understanding these things about anatomy and physiology can be very helpful. There is something very satisfying about living a higher law than many in the world would expect you to live.

Some knowledge of psychology also helps in figuring out boys. How do you know what a boy is thinking? At any moment it is difficult to guess. Millions of random thoughts race through a person's mind every day. Sometimes a boy doesn't really understand what makes him think the way he does. For example, a boy may be wondering if he should ask a particular girl for a date. "What if she says no? What a humiliation," he may think to himself. No one likes to be turned down. So he may not ask the girl out because of the fear of being turned down. Ironically, while he is home with these thoughts, the girl may be waiting anxiously for the phone to ring. It is surprising how many boys and girls sit home and miss activities because someone thought asking would result in a "no" answer.

But suppose the boy gathers the courage and calls. The ringing of the phone seems to go on forever. He thinks about hanging up before anyone answers. Maybe he does. What should he say? What if the girl's father answers? Asking a girl out face to face may be even more difficult, especially if she says no. All these are real problems for a boy.

A boy is also concerned about spiritual and temporal

goals and objectives. Will he be successful? Will he be able to produce enough money for his needs? What's going to happen in his life next year? These questions go on and on. Some boys have goals planned for themselves relatively early in life, while some never do get it all together.

Boys wonder what girls think of them. In fact, a lot of time is spent on this subject by both boys and girls. If a girl is having a difficult time figuring out what a boy is thinking, or why he does and says something, it doesn't hurt to ask. Asking is a good way to find out important things as girls and boys evaluate each other. And it's fun just to talk and get to know people. Another logical question that a girl often thinks about is "How can I get him interested in me?" It may help for her to imagine what things would interest her if she were a boy. Doing and saying those things in the right ways at the right times may take some thought and good judgment. Special boys look for special girls.

It is not coincidence that people with telestial qualities attract one another, while those with celestial qualifications find companions with the same interests and potentials. Your eternal companion is looking for you. How will you recognize each other? How will you know? This is one of the most important questions of your life. The answer will come only through careful thought and prayer.

There's much more to a boy than just anatomy, physiology, and psychology. A boy is a son of God, a person who someday can become an eternal father himself. This may seem a long way off, but that's what life is all about. And that is why it is so important to be in control, always.

How the Sperm Gets There

What can be said about the journey of a lively sperm from father to mother? Everyone knows that a sperm joining an egg may begin the formation of a baby. Everyone knows that a female cannot get pregnant without a sperm from a male, and that a male and female join their bodies to accomplish this. How the sperm gets there is something very special, very sacred, and very private.

The scriptures say that a husband and wife married to each other are to be "one flesh." At such special moments a husband and wife are as close as can be, a part of him within a part of her. The penis of the husband becomes firm and enters her vagina. Millions of sperm are released from the penis into the vagina. Swimming rapidly, in a special fluid, many of these sperm find their way through the cervix up into the uterus. Their speed has been estimated to be between fifteen and twenty miles an hour. They may swim all the way up through the uterus into a fallopian tube. Then, if an ovum is ready, one of the sperm may join it. The fertilized ovum then travels from the fallopian tube into the uterus, where it becomes embedded in the soft uterine lining, the endometrium. The cells grow and divide. An embryo forms and development continues until the baby is ready to be born. From the time the sperm joins the ovum until the birth of the baby, the mother is pregnant.

Does pregnancy always occur when a man and woman have intercourse? No, but without exception the Lord has commanded that this partnership, being "one flesh," is only for a husband and wife married to each other.

Everything about procreation, including one's reproductive organs, deserves great respect and privacy. These parts are not toys. They are to be used only at the right times and in the right circumstances.

The miraculous creation of a little body is too special to joke or talk lightly about. Being one flesh is a commandment. Such times bring great joy for a loving husband and wife. But when this power is misused, heartache and sorrow eventually follow.

Becoming one flesh involves more than pleasure. It means caring, loving, and sharing one another. The joining of bodies may cause excitement and perhaps momentary pleasurable feelings, but without loving, caring, and sharing—and marriage—such pleasure cannot last beyond the moment, and remorse, humiliation, and regret will follow sooner or later.

With love, consideration, and the commitment of marriage, this relationship can be celestial. Day by day, marriage can be the happiest of experiences. One part of this joy and happiness in marriage is the sharing of yourself with someone who belongs to you. Many people mistake sex for love, when sex is really only one part of married love. Many regard playing around with each other's bodies as a game. But many don't know what eternal love is all about. They have confused the real with the counterfeit. The real is celestial. When intimate relationships take place in a celestial way, they can bring pleasure and happiness beyond measure.

Imitation is sometimes so similar to the genuine that it is difficult to tell the difference. Some counterfeit bills look quite real. Sometimes counterfeits of love may seem quite real. Many people never know the difference. A young movie star once commented, "At first I didn't know what love really was . . . but now I know . . . it starts out with plain lust, sometimes growing to liking the guy, and then if it lasts awhile, that's love." It's quite obvious that her idea of love wasn't even a good counterfeit.

But sometimes counterfeits are not so easy to identify. Sometimes two people think they love each other, and they go through the motions of a marital relationship without marriage, rationalizing that it is love. But sex without marriage is always counterfeit. It is something like a fake bill without the backing of a bank or treasury. If you are stuck with a phony twenty-dollar bill, it's your twenty-dollar loss. There is no commitment from anyone to accept it for coins or goods or services. Counterfeit love, sex without marriage, is also without commitment, and it's worse than being cheated with fake money. Twenty dollars is just money. It can be replaced. But virtue, once lost, can never be replaced.

If someone says "Obey the law of chastity," he may think the message has been clear. But five words are not enough. Chastity implies sharing one's body as one flesh only with one's own husband or wife. The joining of a male body and a female body outside of marriage is not acceptable. The joining of two male bodies is not acceptable. The joining of two female bodies is not acceptable. Why? Be-

17

cause this is what the Lord has commanded. And there are many other reasons.

Chastity is special to a person who has it. When a man and a woman love each other very much, one of the ways this love is expressed in marriage is by sharing one another as one flesh. If bodies are shared with just anyone, this expression doesn't mean very much. For people who are married to each other and know that each belongs to the other and no one else, this closeness has special meaning.

Many think that obeying the law of chastity is restrictive and out-of-date. Some rationalize their actions, saying the law of chastity takes away freedom and is too much to expect. But chastity does not take away freedom and is not too much to expect. Obedience to this law opens up freedom—eternal freedom. There is something special about living this law because we want to, not because we have to. There is a special feeling about completely trusting someone we love. There is never a question about "did he . . ." or "I wonder if she . . ."

A person who obeys the law of chastity is in complete control of himself or herself. "Will I?" or "Won't I?" are questions that the person has already answered correctly. Once you've made a decision to obey the law of chastity, the decision never has to be made again. This is a strong defense against temptation. There is a very secure feeling about this protection. When one thinks about the many benefits of chastity right now, it's not necessary to think of the long-range benefits. But when one thinks about eternity, there isn't any doubt at all. To those who want their companions and children forever, chastity should be easy. One of the basic requirements for a forever marriage is chastity. It is very important to have a loving companion who will help us qualify in this requirement and others. It should be obvious how important it is to choose one's marriage companion very carefully.

If we look at all the positive reasons for wanting to live the law of chastity, it's not really necessary to think much about the consequences of not living it. However, those consequences cannot be overlooked. Besides the obvious major consequence of probably not qualifying for the blessings of having an eternal family, and the problem of not being trusted or having the respect of others or yourself, there are still other penalties and problems.

The law of chastity is broken when there is a marital relationship without marriage, whether or not a pregnancy results. The law of chastity is broken whether or not someone gets venereal disease. Even if pregnancy is prevented, sin occurs. Even if disease is prevented, sin occurs. In the many campaigns against venereal disease and pregnancy out of marriage, experts often forget to consider chastity as a solution!

Even with all these campaigns, the incidence of such venereal diseases as gonorrhea and syphilis continues to increase. Why? Are warnings not enough? Why would anyone even consider joining his or her body with someone who is likely to have one of these terrible diseases? Anyone who is willing to have a marital relationship outside of marriage may already have had a similar relationship with someone else, and may already have one or both of these venereal diseases. Who would ever get in a hospital bed with a patient with meningococcus meningitis? No one. Sharing a bed with a person with such dangerous germs would be unthinkable. It would be stupid. Then why would anyone ever consider sharing a bed with someone who may have venereal diseases?

Many people have venereal diseases; in some areas it is almost considered an epidemic. The germs that cause these infections are becoming more and more difficult to control.

Higher doses of antibiotics are needed now to curb them, and some strains are even becoming resistant to antibiotics. But even if antibiotics could conquer all of them, many cases go untreated. The misery and heartache are great. Could a few moments of so-called pleasure be worth such risks?

The world offers many temptations to compromise the law of chastity. How the sperm get where they properly go under the right circumstances is far too sacred a process to tamper with. There are many consequences for playing around with this process. But more important than the consequences are the important reasons *for* chastity: love and obedience.

Chastity is a special gift to give someone after a perfect marriage ceremony. Chastity means sharing your body as one flesh only with your own husband or wife. Chastity is a great quality for you and for someone special who can be your own. Chastity is a priceless possession.

How a
Baby Is
Born

After nine months or so of living protected in a fluid-filled sac in the uterus, a baby is ready to begin a new adventure in the world. Many changes take place quickly. He will breathe oxygen on his own instead of getting it from his mother's blood. He will swallow nourishment on his own instead of obtaining it automatically through the blood vessels of the umbilical cord that connects him to his mother.

Although babies may be in different positions when they are ready to be born, the easiest and the most common position is upside-down. Can you imagine a baby, bottom up and head down, with arms and legs curled around the little body? Sometimes a baby's bottom end is down. This is called a breech position. Other times an arm or leg gets in the way and comes out first, and occasionally a baby slips around sideways, making the delivery difficult. But most of the time things work out perfectly.

About the time the baby is ready to be born, the muscles of the uterus begin to contract, a process that will push the baby out of the uterus. The mother feels this squeezing and tightening of the muscles of the uterus. There is a rest period, and then the contraction occurs again. As the contractions become more frequent, the

mother is usually taken to a hospital where she can be made comfortable during the birth of the baby. At the hospital she is checked to make sure that the baby is all right and everything is proceeding normally. Monitors keep track of the heart rate of the baby and the contractions of the mother.

As the muscles of the uterus contract, the opening of the uterus, which is the cervix, begins to get bigger. Imagine the uterus as an enlarged, hollowed-out upside-down pear. The opening, or cervix, is at the bottom. When this opening becomes about nine centimeters in size, the baby can come through. When the baby is upside-down, as is usually the case, the head begins to push through first. As the mother lies on her back, with her knees up, she pushes. The uterus contracts and the cervix opens wide enough for the baby's head (or bottom) to push through. The baby then pushes through the vagina with everything stretching so it can pass through. The little head turns, and then the shoulders, and out he or she comes. Beautiful. Just beautiful!

There is nothing more exciting or more wonderful than the miracle of birth. And that's just the beginning of many new adventures ahead for parents who will love and care for their very own little boy or girl.

Sometimes the script changes a little. Having twins or triplets (or more) may be even more exciting. Occasionally a baby must be born by caesarean section, an operation through the abdomen, which often saves the life of the baby. But more often, a baby will be born through the natural process, and usually everything is all right.

Every birth is a miracle. Every new baby is precious. But nothing can compare with the experience of seeing and holding your own little miracle for the first time, unless it's the second, or third, or fourth, or fifth, or sixth, or . . .

Masturbation

With a partner, you have the fantastic power to parent children. The scriptures make it clear that being one flesh with a marriage partner is good. But masturbation is counterfeit. It is degrading. It is unwholesome. It causes loss of dignity. And, of greatest concern, masturbation causes loss of the Spirit.

Masturbation is a fake. It tricks a person's body into imitating a husband-wife relationship. In the male, sperm and seminal fluid are made to discharge. As this happens, the body is further fooled into thinking more sperm are needed, and more are produced. Each time masturbation occurs, the problem increases as it becomes more of a habit, intensified by a thought and action cycle.

It is also wrong for girls to masturbate. In the female also, self-stimulation creates an increase in feelings that are difficult to control. These particular feelings in both male and female are intended to be experienced in marriage, where they serve an important purpose, bringing husband and wife together.

Masturbation

Suppose a boy happens to inherit an expensive automobile. Imagine that the car is in the garage. The key is there, but the car is not licensed because the new owner does not yet have a driver's license. It's his car and he has the key. He may even know how to drive. But if he does use the car, serious consequences may occur. Unless both car and driver are legally licensed, driving may result in penalties.

Timing in the use of one's reproductive power is much more important than timing in the use of a car. As this sacred power is used, a husband and wife are brought together through a complex sequence of feelings. In marriage these feelings have purpose. Without marriage they are like wanting to drive a car without a license. Driving without a license could result in a fine or perhaps loss of the car. Using one's power of procreation without marriage could result in severe penalties that may last forever.

The sex desire can be normal, natural, and wholesome, depending on what you do with it. Those who want a forever marriage control these feelings and urges until marriage when the desire can be used in its intended way. However, since such feelings are a natural process, from time to time thoughts and desires will come when their use is inappropriate. A momentary thought is not necessarily a great transgression, but dwelling on such a thought or acting on it might be.

A temple marriage is too precious to risk missing. You probably decided long ago to save these feelings, urges, and this greatest expression of physical love for your own special someone when you are married. Great. Don't let anyone, at any time, under any circumstances, convince you otherwise. Masturbation is wrong. Stimulating one's own sexual powers into action is not wholesome or good. But the situation is even uglier if masturbation progresses another step. When two people of the same sex become involved in masturbation together, or in any way join bodies sexually, this is homosexuality. It is not an illness, and it is not inherited. Homosexuality is a sin.

But what about the feelings one has even when no one else is around? This is a very real problem. Masturbation is a common habit. Because it is common, many rationalize that there is nothing wrong with it. In fact, writers, psychologists, and other so-called experts frequently suggest that it is good. It seems as though whenever a particular behavior becomes somewhat common, there is a clamor to call it normal.

Someone thought up a sales pitch once that said, "Forty thousand Frenchmen can't be wrong." Someone might just as well say "ten million Americans can't be wrong," or "a hundred million Russians can't be wrong." It doesn't take much thought to realize that such conclusions don't have any validity. Of course forty thousand or even a hundred million people could be wrong—and often *are* wrong about a particular thing. Something is not true just because a lot of people think it is. In some cases, a great majority might be wrong. Throughout history this has happened many times, in different circumstances, cultures, and civilizations. So it doesn't matter if a lot of psychologists, or doctors, or anyone else all say that masturbation is good. It isn't.

Very specific instructions have been given by the prophets about this transgression. Masturbation is considered serious enough that a person who has had this problem and who has not repented cannot receive a temple recommend, go on a mission, or be married in the temple until complete repentance occurs. The Spirit of the Lord cannot be with a person who is involved in sin. However, these restrictions and consequences are not permanent, providing there is repentance.

Masturbation

Masturbation is a repentable transgression. But for the special blessings of priesthood advancements, temple privileges, and eternal marriage, a person must be in control of his or her body. These special blessings require the Spirit of the Lord.

Suppose a person has had this problem and perhaps has not realized the seriousness of it. Usually when this awareness occurs, a person feels absolutely terrible. Maybe totally humiliated is a better description. What can a person do? At this point it is essential to stop immediately. Boy or girl, the answer is the same—stop. The longer the problem continues, the more difficult it becomes. So stopping now is a giant step in solving this problem, and avoiding other problems that might occur.

Since control of *actions* begins with control of *thoughts,* this is where controlling the problem of masturbation begins—by carefully selecting what thoughts are allowed in one's mind. It's not always easy to do this. Sometimes a negative thought just pops in. Even when one has no intention at all of doing or thinking anything wrong, something in the environment may trigger such a thought. Pictures, advertisements, stories, television shows, movies, and comments are just a few of the possible origins of negative thoughts. Since some environments increase the likelihood of exposing one's mind to immoral thoughts or ideas, where we are and what we see makes a difference.

But what about the ugly thought that gets there anyway? The answer has to do with how long we let the thought linger. If we don't have a plan for eliminating it, the thought will probably stay there for a while, with one thought leading to another. Dwelling upon these thoughts often lead to undesirable ideas and actions.

A plan to stop this chain reaction must involve a way to erase a bad thought as soon as it starts. One way to do this is to have a substitute good thought waiting to take its place. In baseball, the substitute relief pitcher has to be warmed up. In the thought process a substitute thought is often needed. What kind of thought might be a good substitute? Perhaps remembering the happiest day of your life. Perhaps thinking of a certain scripture, or thinking about going to the temple would be a good way to crowd out spurious thoughts. Some people think about the words of a favorite hymn or song. Maybe a reserve thought could be about plans for a special trip or project. Choose your own substitute thought now, and keep it warmed up in reserve. Then use it when it is needed to help erase a bad thought. And once thoughts are controlled, so are actions.

An essential part of repenting of a problem such as masturbation is to talk about it with one's priesthood leader. This means talking with one's bishop, branch president, or perhaps mission president. Unpleasant as this may seem, it must be done. Even though it may seem impossible to tell him what has been going on, it isn't. Every bishop has talked to many others with this problem. It is solvable—but delay makes it worse, adding a lot of worry and concern.

A very fine young man agonized about this for weeks before he gained the courage to say anything. But he did. And after his visit, he wished he had done so much sooner. He gained the confidence needed to control his feelings, emotions, and body, and he did control them. Incidentally, this young man has several boys of his own now, and is a bishop who has helped numerous young people with this same problem.

A delightful young woman was also tormented with this problem. Somehow she got started. It didn't happen very often, but it happened. She thought she knew it wasn't right to excite those special body parts that way, and she was disturbed about it, but she didn't know what to do. Then one day her mother walked in and realized what was going on. The girl was red-faced and tearful. How embarrassing! But the next hour changed everything. She and her mother talked. There was a lot of love and understanding in that visit. The next Sunday, she slipped quietly into the bishop's office between meetings. She didn't do very well at holding back the tears, and some big ones rolled down her cheeks, but somehow she got out the words, explaining that she had been having the problem, but that it was over and there wouldn't be a next time.

Even worse difficulties can occur when the problem of self-abuse is covered up and not admitted when a bishop asks about it. Sometimes this occurs in the case of a missionary who knows exactly what masturbation is. He may be terribly ashamed. He may want to stop and may do well for a while. But the problem is compounded by saying there is no problem when one is asked about it. A missionary with this problem will find it difficult to accomplish his work, because he cannot be in tune with the Spirit. Such a circumstance should never get to this point. The problem should have been talked about, repented of, and cleared long before a person goes on a mission.

As the missionary seeks the help of his priesthood leaders, repentance may then be possible and successful work accomplished. But valuable time will have been lost because of the sin, multiplied by untruthfulness. How much better it is never to begin this troublesome habit. And how much better it is when it does occur that one get it cleared up immediately—without delay.

For those who have never had a problem with the degrading habit of masturbation, don't begin. Do everything possible to keep yourself thinking and doing what you will be pleased about tomorrow and the next day. Avoid everything that would cause your thoughts to drift to unclean actions, such as sexually stimulating stories, movies, and conversations. Spending too much time alone is unwise. Activities, prayer, and filling your mind with good thoughts can all help.

Why is masturbation a problem? Because masturbation means a person is not in control. It is an act of misusing a very special and sacred power. Masturbation is an ugly, selfish expression of emotion. And as it becomes habit-forming it may lead to more serious transgressions involving one's body and the sacred power of procreation. This habit can be overcome and should be, right now, if it is a problem. But if it has not been a problem, an excellent commitment would be to never, ever, let it happen, even once.

D-E-F-E-N-S-E

Sometimes hands get where they should not be. Sometimes there is a vicious immoral attack. At other times things happen when boys and girls think they are just playing around. Something immoral may happen in a car, at home, or in a million other places. The persons involved may be on a date. The problem could be caused by an older person, possibly even a friend of the family or a relative. This may seem incredible, but it happens sometimes.

The person with unclean ideas might be someone of the same sex! Disgusting? Worse than that. Or the person may be of the opposite sex. Still intolerable. No matter who it happens to be, boy or girl, man or woman, friend or stranger, don't let anything happen. Stop the action. Don't let anyone ever put a hand on you where it should not be, or ever try to loosen your clothing or do anything that violates the privacy of your body.

But it is possible that something like this could begin to happen. It could start by being too close to someone special. It could happen when you least expect it. Whatever

the circumstance, be prepared. Knowing how to prevent loss of virtue may be even more important than knowing how to save a life. Drowning, choking, electrocutions, and poisonings all require immediate action to prevent things from rapidly getting completely out of control. If the right thing isn't done immediately, serious consequences may occur, even death.

One of the basic principles in first aid is prevention. This is also vital in preserving moral cleanliness and chastity.

Being morally clean means thinking and acting in such ways that the law of chastity is kept. Being morally clean implies being in complete control of one's body and its reproductive capabilities. Being morally clean requires a higher degree of self-control and self-mastery than most people realize. Let's put these thoughts into some very straight language:

A boy or man should not cause himself or anyone else, male or female, to be sexually stimulated or allow anyone to sexually stimulate him, other than in a marriage relationship.

A girl or woman should not cause herself or anyone else, male or female, to be sexually stimulated or allow anyone to sexually stimulate her, other than in a marriage relationship.

If any more clarity is needed, being morally clean means this: No one should touch, fondle, or fool around with his or her own or anyone else's private body parts, including those parts of the body between the legs of boys and girls and the breast areas of girls. These areas are too private to be touched or tampered with.

You can probably avoid all these problems by being in the right places at the right times, under the right circumstances. Choosing good friends helps. Avoiding being alone with someone for a long period of time makes good sense. Life is often a combination of choices and risks and

33

chances, and no one is safe from the possibility of getting into a situation that may result in serious consequences.

But what if someone does get too close? This may happen in a way that may seem quite innocent, especially when a couple have been with one another quite a bit. The more friendly a boy and girl become and the more time they spend together, the more likely it is that a problem could develop. This is so even when they are looking ahead to a temple marriage. When there is too much closeness, and feelings start getting out of control, someone needs to say "stop!" It helps to talk. It helps more to pray about it. It helps even more to exercise self-discipline and say goodnight.

But what if you are out on a date and someone starts doing something that doesn't seem right? Usually by expressing disapproval at the very beginning you can stay in control. Don't let things progress—not at all. Take whatever defensive action is needed. It's probably time to end the date, or at least to go where other people are—perhaps home.

If things don't get stopped, more and more closeness and touching may occur. These intimacies should be reserved for marriage because they create feelings and excitement that may be much more rapidly progressive than ever intended.

No matter how romantic it all seems, no matter what line is used, exciting one another's bodies outside a marriage relationship is wrong. Such actions can quickly lead to total loss of chastity. This kind of touching can lead to "going all the way," which means sexual intimacy reserved for husband and wife. Even when touching and playing around does not result in "going all the way," these are serious transgressions that must be repented of and cleared with one's bishop before priesthood advancement or temple privileges may be given.

Sometimes an attempt is made to do more than touch or fondle a person's body. Forcing a sexual relationship is called rape. This is one of the most offensive of all crimes. Prevention is the best defense against it. When you are in safe places and circumstances, the likelihood of rape diminishes greatly, which is why a girl or woman should not go out alone, especially at night. In many circumstances it is even dangerous for two girls to be out alone. Sometimes it is difficult to anticipate the circumstances in which such a terrible crime might be attempted, so good judgment and common sense are extremely important.

If someone attempts such an attack, what should you do? Fight! Resist! Yell loudly! Use every possible means to defend yourself! This is one circumstance when almost any means of disabling, disarming, or hurting the attacker would be justified. This might include a fist in the face, a kick in the stomach or groin, throwing salt or pepper in the eyes, or doing anything imaginable that could stop the attacker. Then run. Scream, yell, and get to the safest place you can think of. Do whatever is possible to identify the person and report what has happened. Such vicious criminals must be stopped.

Knowing some facts about rape can be a helpful protection. Rapes don't all happen in dark alleys. Many, probably most of them, are planned. In fact, about half of all rapes occur in the victim's own home! The horrible message is that any girl or woman can be raped, anywhere, anytime. But studies have shown that a few important precautions will usually prevent rape from occurring.

At home, keep all the doors and windows locked, especially when you're alone. Drapes or blinds should cover windows at night. Better still, try not to be home or anywhere else alone.

Never give personal information to a stranger. Sometimes people who call on the phone or who come to the door can be very convincing. Still the rule is sound. Giving personal information to strangers is unwise, even when they seem friendly.

When walking, avoid being alone on dark streets or on any street that might not be safe. Avoid alleys and places with dark doorways and unlit parking lots, and never accept a ride from a stranger. All these things involve much too great a risk.

When you are going someplace in a car, always lock it and secure the windows. Have your keys ready when you return to the car, and check behind the front seats to be absolutely sure no one is hiding there. Of course, it's best to never be out alone, even in a car.

And what about clothing? Some kinds of clothing may appear suggestive and provoke a deviant into action. Crime prevention experts also caution girls and women to avoid wearing tight skirts and dresses and high heels that could slow down running if it should be necessary.

What can you do if you think you are in danger? Yell. Scream. Make a noise. Blow a whistle or shake a noisemaker. Rapists and hoodlums hate loud noises that attract attention. If you are pursued and no one hears your shouts for help, it might be necessary to do something as radical as breaking someone's window to attract attention.

Experts have found that the best defense against attack is to quickly do something to surprise the attacker. If you have something in your hand, such as a handbag, swing it at his face and run. A handful of pepper thrown in an attacker's face is very distracting. Of course, most people don't walk around with pepper in their hands, but this isn't a bad idea, if walking in questionable circumstances is necessary. Biting, scratching, or kicking might not be fair in any other situation, but they are in this one. A well-placed kick to the attacker's groin can be disabling. Then run. Don't try to argue with or overpower an attacker, just do something to quickly distract him and get away fast!

If such an experience occurs, it is most comforting to share the problem with someone who cares, such as a mother, father, or bishop. At a time like this, a person needs someone who understands. It's no kindness to others to let a rape or attempted rape go by without doing everything that can be done to prevent it from happening again. A person who attempts immoral acts with one person will try again. The only way for this to be stopped is to be sure someone who can do something knows about it.

There are many situations that are morally unsafe. Avoiding such situations is the best defense and the best protection you can have.

What If...

Let's suppose a city had a big problem with traffic violations, mostly speeding. There were so many tickets being issued that the city was getting a bad reputation. Then someone came up with the solution that fewer speeders should be stopped and fewer tickets issued. This didn't stop the speeding, but it made the record look better. Then things really got out of hand. There were more speeders than ever. Since the local police were ignoring the violations, the state police began issuing tickets—and again there were far too many tickets.

Finally it was assumed that speeding was inevitable, a fact of life. Pamphlets were printed, special classes were set up in schools, radio and TV campaigns were started, and offices opened to provide people with information— information on how to avoid speeding tickets! Various methods were discussed in detail, including the use of radar detectors, CB radios, and large rearview mirrors. Free equipment was offered to those who could not pay, because of the great importance of reducing the number of speeding tickets. Of course, *not* speeding was never discussed as a solution. Speeding was such an established way of life that avoiding it would not be practical. The programs and organizations sponsoring this no-ticket-for-speeding campaign were largely supported by tax dollars.

And one more thing—should anyone happen to get a ticket, even with all these precautions, more help was available. Special headquarters were set up in all parts of the city to function as ticket-fixing centers. Various legal maneuvers were available, but at these centers, if nothing else worked the ticket was destroyed by burning.

Ridiculous? Yes, this scenario is as ridiculous as can be, but much of the same shallow reasoning is used in campaigns for birth control. With banners waving about stopping the problem of pregnancies among the unmarried, people and institutions study and discuss various methods of avoiding these pregnancies. Free equipment and supplies are passed out, and instructions are carefully given, all with the goal of preventing pregnancies. No one mentions chastity. It's out of date. It isn't practical. The so-called experts expect the young and old alike to be immoral.

Radio and television campaigns encourage birth control. Magazines, newspaper articles, posters, pamphlets, lectures, and often school classes teach about it. Over and over the message is given: "Avoid pregnancy by using birth control." Pills, sperm-killing medicines, shots, and surgery are used. Much so-called sex education is directed toward teaching students about birth control and how to practice it. Much propaganda is directed toward avoiding unwanted children.

Of course, no one wants any girl to become pregnant without marriage. A baby needs two parents. A family is very important. It is sad for an unmarried girl to become pregnant, but is birth control the answer? Some important considerations have been missed.

Apparently some experts haven't thought of the idea of chastity. Rather than propaganda about birth control, why not talk about chastity? Chastity solves the problem of pregnancy outside of marriage. Chastity also solves the problem of venereal disease, which birth control pills and injections do not. And chastity solves and prevents a mountain of other problems.

A woman doctor with much charisma spoke at a medical meeting about the importance of birth control for adolescents. She listed a full page of side effects of birth control pills, including nausea, bloating, weight gain, breakthrough bleeding, hypertension, thrombophlebitis, epilepsy, oligomenorrhea, collagen disease, diabetes, jaundice, eye problems, depression, possibly cancer, and occasionally even death. She then asked, "How could anyone prescribe the pill with all these side effects?" Her answer was, "Well, when you're talking about adolescents, there just isn't much choice."

What a statement to make! What she apparently meant was that in choosing a form of birth control for adolescents, in her opinion there wasn't much choice. She did make a list that included abstinence (not having sexual relations), but this was not seriously considered and was rapidly dismissed as being impractical. To this doctor and to many other persons, the foregone conclusion is that there is going to be sexual activity among young people before marriage. To her, even with all the risks of the pill, there was no choice.

We have more confidence in youth than this. No matter what some may think, or what some statistics may show about others, you are different. You have higher values. You know who you are. You have an idea about where you are going. You are on your way to a successful life and eternity with your forever family.

But as you think about where you are, and of all your blessings, be thankful your parents invited you to be here. Some years ago, when a particular sperm and egg met, your earthly body began. Consider some of the things that could have happened.

As your tiny body began to form, a vacuumlike instrument could have dislodged it and swept it away. Surgical instruments or other methods could have also ended that pregnancy. What an awful thought!

Two words describe abortion: *ugly* and *selfish*. Yet it's talked about as an everyday occurrence among unmarried girls who become pregnant, and is even sometimes advocated as a means of limiting the size of families.

With so many abortions, couples who cannot have children of their own often find it impossible to adopt a baby. People call our office frequently with the same question: "Can't you help us find a baby to adopt?" Unfortunately, the answer too often is "probably not."

Often propaganda about contraception and abortion says "every child should be wanted." The implication is that if a child isn't wanted, an abortion might as well be done. Yes, every child should be wanted. Every baby *is* wanted. Finding a home for a baby is no problem. With so many abortions being done, there are few babies available to be adopted, and the waiting lists of couples who want babies and cannot have them get longer.

A girl told us about her experience with an abortion. "It's something I am never going to forget," she said, as tears rolled down her cheeks. "Friends said it wasn't going to be a big deal, but it was. The nightmares, the guilt feelings—I'll never get over this, never."

Every time she tells her story she breaks into tears. At other times hearing a baby's laugh or squeal will bring this horrible experience to mind and she sobs some more. If you were to ask her about abortion, she would tell you as she has told many others: "Don't."

But what about an unmarried girl who finds that she is pregnant? What should she do? And what about the baby's father?

A pretty girl and a tall boy sat in our office staring at the floor. She started to say something, but the words wouldn't come out. Finally after some long pauses, she stammered, "How early can you tell if someone is pregnant?" After her question was answered it was apparent she was the "someone," and a test confirmed that she was pregnant.

The story that unfolded was all too common. They didn't think this was going to happen. "How am I going to tell my mom, let alone my dad?" she asked. She replied without waiting for an answer, "I'll just tell them . . ." The boy didn't say much—she did most of the talking.

The girl and her family had been our good friends for many years. We had been through infections, skiing accidents, and a serious head injury together over the years. "What's going to happen to us—will we be excommunicated from the Church?" she wanted to know. "Is there ever a chance to have an eternal marriage after this?" Her mind was filled with questions, thoughts, and worries. Suddenly this beautiful, carefree girl and her boyfriend had a million problems. He looked troubled, but it was more than a worried expression. What color had been in his face when they had arrived was now gone. He was as pale as someone who has just witnessed a terrible accident.

She was a lovely girl and a good student. No one who knew her would have ever thought that something like this would happen. There had been just one night together. She knew she should have never let him be there. It was even more obvious now. He knew better too. But it happened—just once—and now this.

But now what? How would you have answered her questions? Once the couple realized that all this was happening, they knew some decisions had to be made. They quickly ruled out abortion; she knew she couldn't do that. The next step was to get all the help they could. Her parents were much more understanding than she had thought they might be. Of course they were disappointed. But like hundreds of times before, when smaller things were involved, they were there when their daughter needed them. Her dad loved her very much. So did her mom.

The family talked almost all that night. As they talked about decisions to be made, the bishop dropped in to offer what help he could. They realized the main problem came down to two choices: she could either give the baby up for adoption, or she and the boy could get married. The boy thought they should get married right away. He felt responsible for the whole problem. They thought they loved each other. Maybe it would all work out. They read from the scriptures, particularly Exodus 22:16 and Deuteronomy 22:28-29.

The bishop explained about church courts and the penalties of disfellowshipment and excommunication. He explained that church courts are held with love and a sincere desire to help. Before this the couple had had no idea that church courts helped people clear transgressions.

During the weeks and months that followed these young people learned a lot about the law of repentance. Many problems came up, expected and unexpected. They knew that many in their circumstances would never make it, but they were determined that they would. Statistically the risks were not very good. But they knew they could count on their parents and their bishop for help. They

really wanted priesthood and temple blessings for life and eternity. It was all up to them.

If ever there is a problem about transgression concerning the laws of morality or chastity (or any other law), it is extremely important to get the matter cleared and resolved. Part of this process must include a willingness to confess the transgression to one's bishop; to honestly and sincerely put the transgression behind, resolving never to do the thing again; and to follow through with such a resolution.

Repentance is not easy, but it is possible, and is the *only* way back. If a transgression occurs, there are two possible directions to go: one can either make the problem worse, or one can do everything possible to get back on a celestial road. If ever you find yourself near the edge of that road, or off even a little, talk to your bishop. Likewise, if there is ever any question about these sacred matters, your bishop can help you find the right answer. He can provide comfort, counsel, and wise direction through inspiration and direction from the Lord.

As you look ahead to your marriage, make it celestial. Disregard the popular clamor for birth control. Follow the words of the prophets about having many children, and don't put having a family off for worldly expenses.

In a world where many delight in living according to the doctrines of men, especially where abortion and birth control are so popular, the words of a little boy saying his prayers echo loudly: "Heavenly Father, thank thee for mommy, 'cause she let me be born."

"It Is Easier to Remember . . ."

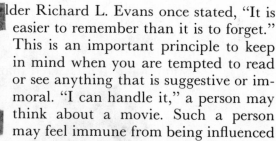

lder Richard L. Evans once stated, "It is easier to remember than it is to forget." This is an important principle to keep in mind when you are tempted to read or see anything that is suggestive or immoral. "I can handle it," a person may think about a movie. Such a person may feel immune from being influenced or affected by a not-so-good show. And going is often easier than trying to convince friends to do something else. But what about the effect? Can a single show influence us?

Suppose the movie begins with some breathtakingly beautiful photography of the inland waterways off the coast of British Columbia. It may seem worth the ticket price just to see the white water breaking into millions of droplets against majestically jagged rocks with white clouds in a blue sky. What could be wrong with such a movie? Then, after more beautiful scenes, there is an air view of a luxury cruiser slipping smoothly through a narrow inland passage. The camera zooms in on the ship and pans the bridge, the deck, the swimming pool, and a row of passenger cabins. The next sequence is inside one of the

cabins. And suddenly the screen is no longer filled with the beautiful scenery, but with explicit scenes in that cabin. The visual impact is sordid, and not as interesting as one might imagine.

Anyone who has witnessed something horrible finds it difficult, if not impossible, to ever completely erase it from memory. It's as though the experience is videotaped and replayed from time to time, often when the person doesn't even want to think about it.

But what about the everyday shows and stories about people who become involved in immorality? Even without explicit sex scenes on the screen, often little is left to the imagination. Sometimes immoral situations are added to otherwise good stories to sell books or increase ticket sales. This makes finding a movie without immorality difficult. One cannot escape the fact that exposure to these things may be permanently recorded in the mind.

Another problem is what happens to one's sensitivities and feelings about immoral situations that are repeatedly visualized. If nothing else, immoral actions become common everyday occurrences—without causing surprise, shock, or disgust. Consciously or subconsciously, the idea grows. The more common something seems, the more accepted it may become. Seeing immorality depicted in day-to-day situations is a distraction and diversion from celestial thoughts. Behavior may not change, at least not right away, but attitudes can change, little by little, and at some point in time, behavior may follow.

But what about just one movie? We often don't realize just what effect a book or program or show really does have. There is an effect—and often it is powerful. A complex series of factors is involved, one of which relates to why we select what we will see or read for diversion. Almost everyone gets tired of his or her daily routine, at least once in a while. A nurse gets tired of being a nurse. A student gets tired of being a student. A teacher gets tired of being a teacher. No matter what one's job is, a change of pace is sometimes needed.

If we choose to watch a television program, read a book, or go to a show, we may soon become absorbed in the story and escape for a little while from our day-to-day routine. One can stop being a student and forget his concerns and worries while his feet are propped up and he is reading a novel. He can forget for a while his own concerns and worries. Likewise, at a show one imagines how it is to be the hero or heroine. It might be rather fun to trade roles for a little while. This happens just about every time we go to a show. But whom are we trading places with? There is quite a difference between the feelings and attitudes we have as we put ourselves into the role of a prophet compared with those we have when we put ourselves into the part of a hero who has just committed adultery or a heroine who is a prostitute. The more vividly we identify with a character, the more effect the experience may have. Sometimes this may be difficult to control. In sinful situations, the more explicitly the male-female physical relationships are portrayed, the greater may be the problem to the viewer or reader. The scriptures tell us that "whosoever looketh on a woman to lust after her hath committed adultery with her already in his heart." (Matthew 5:28.)

Shows and books often leave little out. Often the leading characters are involved in negative and immoral behavior in ways that are made to seem desirable. The message is that "serious relationships" outside of marriage are now acceptable—and somehow everything works out. Many see, read about, and live these situations vicariously—and believe the message. Most don't realize how subtly these things happen, how everything we see and hear does affect us, often changing our thinking without our even realizing it.

What if all the shows in town are losers? What if a group of friends decides to go to a questionable show? Or what about a date? What if you had to choose between going to a bad show or staying home? No one likes to be left out. No one likes to miss a good time with friends. It comes down to risks and benefits. The benefits may seem big and the risks may seem small, unless there is perception and maturity. It isn't easy to explain that a particular show doesn't meet our standards, but such an explanation will almost always be respected. Even when taunting comments are made by a group, a person's esteem goes up when principles are set and kept.

What if all the shows are questionable? Don't go. There is always something better to do. Finding that something may take considerable thought and ingenuity. But it's worth making memories that are good rather than those that may cause us problems, and that later we would rather forget.

Another problem is how we dress and the effect of our dress selection on others.

Some boys were overheard talking about girls in skimpy swimsuits: "I was really embarrassed!" "I don't think girls realize what it does to a guy when they look like that."

Finding decent swimwear is sometimes almost impossible. Looking through a catalogue can be a shock. Going to the beach or pool may be worse. Sometimes other clothing fashions pose the same dilemmas. Some clothes are purposely made to be too tight, or too skimpy, or too translucent or even transparent. Some of these fashions may seem lovely, but the problem is the effect such ex-

posure may have on others.

Often girls have no idea how boys' impulses and desires are stirred up and stimulated at inappropriate times, and how difficult self-control becomes. Girls usually just want to be attractive, but sometimes they do more than just attract attention.

Suggestive clothing on the beach, at a pool, at school, or on a date may communicate ideas without anything being said or done. Tight, skimpy, or see-through clothing sends a certain message to every male around. The message may be conveyed without the girl's having any idea or intention of sending it, but innocently or not, the message is transmitted.

Is the choice of clothing important? Does it matter? Does it make a difference? Yes. But how does anyone find modest clothing? Where can one find a swimsuit that doesn't show so much that immoral thoughts are stimulated? These are tough questions. The easiest thing to do is to wear the fashions that are most available. Most people do this. But most people probably don't realize who they are and don't have any idea about their eternal potential. Most people will not have a choice, faithful partner for a lifetime. Most people will not have a loving eternal companion. Most people just don't realize the long-range consequences of a skimpy swimsuit or of see-through clothing.

When popular styles are not modest, some girls make their own clothing and even swimwear. Sometimes a lining or other additions or alterations can transform an immodest outfit into one that is attractive but modest. Good solutions, although difficult, will be found by a few. The ones who do find these solutions are probably on their way to qualifying for a marriage that will last forever.

What we see on the screen and in real life does affect us. The effect is more than momentary and for the present, because what we see, read, and hear is stored in memory in our computer-like brains. But there is a difference between our brains and a computer. When something is stored in a computer memory, the "memory-clear" key can erase the stored data. This is not so easy with things stored in our brains. Sometimes it is easier to remember than it is to forget. Not allowing undesirable influences to be recorded in the first place is best. But this is not easy. Saying no about a show and avoiding other suggestive situations and influences takes the best of good judgment and control.

Parents

Suppose you have just returned from a military patrol along a trail loaded with booby traps and land mines. The slightest wrong steps have triggered deadly explosions, and only two of the nine in your patrol have returned. After such an experience you would certainly want to warn the next patrol about the mines and how to avoid them.

Your parents feel somewhat like this. They worry as you follow them along the booby-trapped trail. Sometimes it doesn't seem that there is a problem. But the mines are well hidden. You probably feel quite safe and have a good feeling about avoiding problems, and your parents probably have a lot of confidence in you. But they don't trust the mines. They know it's difficult to see them all. They hope and pray you will. Since you are absolutely sure you can make it, sometimes it's hard to imagine why they are concerned. You probably know your parents so well you can predict what they will do and say about a lot of things. You know that they worry about friends who may distract you, and sometimes they may react strongly to something that seems harmless to you. From time to time they see a mine, or think they do, that might cause them to say no to a pretty simple request.

Parents can't always convincingly explain why they feel the way they do about a decision. Maybe they just have a feeling—call it inspiration, intuition, or whatever you want. Sometimes, of course, parents make mistakes. But parents have a good enough batting average to count on their being right most of the time even if their suggestions don't seem logical at a particular moment.

One of the things that worries parents most is where you are and whom you are with. Remembering their own experiences as they grew up, they may worry some more. They would like to save you from the traps they almost fell into.

Although dating seems like a harmless sport, there are many risks. As you think about these risks, it's easier to see why parents are so concerned about the friends their children are with. When it comes to cars and to dating, dads are particularly concerned. This is a characteristic of fathers. So if your dad is very protective and likes it better when you are home, this is a rather normal fatherly feeling and attitude. His concern increases greatly under some circumstances. That's why he wants to know where you are going, who is driving, who will be there, and when you will be back. If occasionally you get the feeling he doesn't trust you, keep in mind that it's a dad's business to keep informed about his children.

If someone were to come along wanting to borrow your dad's new car, what would he say? Suppose this car was worth many thousands of dollars. Suppose he had waited a long time to get it. Suppose he liked it so much that he kept it spotlessly clean, dusting and polishing it every day. Then someone asks him to just hand over the car keys. If your dad really were generous enough to loan out his new car, do you think he would hand over the keys without knowing where that person wanted to take it? Don't you think he would want to find out a little bit about the person who was going to be driving? Don't you think he'd want to know if he had a good driving record? Don't you think he would want to know when the car would be back? Don't you think he would want to make some suggestions about taking care of his car? Don't you think he would want to know who else would be going along? If your dad really were going to loan his new car, he would probably want to know all these things—and maybe some more. This would be entirely reasonable.

A dad probably wants to know the same kinds of things about someone who is taking out his daughter as he wants to know about someone who is borrowing his car. He may even want to know more! After all, if he were to loan out the car and it was totally wrecked, he might lose thousands of dollars, but if something were to happen to his son or daughter, the consequences could be eternal. The value of a car is nothing compared to the value of someone as important as you.

Traffic accidents are all too common, and they cause inconvenience, suffering, or even death. But parents are even more concerned about a possible moral tragedy. So it's important to them, even though they trust you, to know something about everyone you date. Second-hand information is not enough. When your parents get to know your friends, they will worry a lot less. Invite your friends to your house. Spend time there around your parents. The better your parents know your friends, the more confidence they can usually have.

If a boy doesn't like the idea of meeting a girl's parents and visiting a little with her father when he comes to take her out, there is a good chance he has a problem. A boy who hasn't a very good track record or whose intentions are not very good will probably be reluctant to talk with a girl's father. And when the word gets around that a girl's dad talks to the boys who take her out, the less-than-desirable boys usually don't come around. A really desirable boy doesn't mind visiting with a girl's dad. He respects her all the more, and is more careful than ever about taking good care of her. A boy's dad also needs to know something about the girls his son takes out and about their goings and comings.

The dating and courtship years are exciting. Your dad and mom can help these years go by successfully and safely.

Remember about the booby traps and land mines—they are real. Loving parents can help you miss them. And they will, if you let them.

Parents want everything to work out perfectly for their children—no skateboard falls, no car accidents, no disappointments, no mistakes, no sickness, no trouble—only happiness and success. Of course, it can't always be that way. Everyone has to do a lot of learning through the experience of making some mistakes and having some bumps and problems.

But many of these bumps and problems, like the land mines, can be avoided, with the help of parents who have been through it before.

Parents can be remarkable friends. They can be some of the best friends you ever have. If it hasn't been quite that way, it can be. How? In the same way any friend becomes your special friend—by your being a special friend yourself. Let them share your joys and your troubles. Confide in them and help them understand the things you do and the way you feel. By talking about things, you will make this easier for them. With understanding, communication, and caring, a very special friendship will grow that can last forever.

Friends

Everyone needs friends. In fact, having friends is so important all sorts of things are done to attract them.

One young boy went through his house each morning stealing money from purses, wallets, and drawers. The missing money created all sorts of upsets in the family, as might be expected, but it kept disappearing for a long time before the boy was caught. What was he doing with the loot, which added up to several dollars each day? Each morning at school he gave away money, mostly coins, but sometimes one-dollar and five-dollar bills. Incredibly, he wanted friends so badly that he tried to buy them.

Other precious things are given away by people who try to buy friendship. A girl may want a friend so much that she may let a boy touch her and play with her like a toy. Eventually she may even give her most precious possession of all, her virtue. What kind of friendship could be bought this way? Certainly not one that would last very long.

A boy may give away his chastity in hopes of pleasing a

girl, again trying to buy friendship. These kinds of friendships are worthless. There is no trust, no confidence, no love. "If he does this with me, who else does he do it with?" the girl wonders, and the boy feels the same emptiness about her. In the meantime their virtue has been spent—lost forever in a search for friendships that could never work.

People do rather strange things when they are trying to win friends. Often they compete to get in the spotlight of attention. This may work if that spotlight involves positive actions. But what about a little boy who pulls a girl's hair? Sometimes children tease one another about being too heavy or too small, about the size of ears, or countless other things. Such cruelty isn't limited to little children; teenagers also do a lot of putting-down, and, amazingly, so do adults. Whether the put-down is about a person's big ears, or slowness to understand math, or mistakes at the office, no one likes to be made to appear foolish.

Why would anyone try to make another person appear stupid? Apparently a person thinks that by pushing another person *down,* he or she is put *up.* Could this ever win popularity? Putting people down is like the childish "king-of-the-mountain" game where the object is to knock everyone else off the hill. The one on the top is the king. In order to stay on top, he bumps off anyone else who tries to get up. Putting everyone else down doesn't make the king very popular: in fact, the longer he stays on top of the hill the more anxious everyone else becomes to knock him down.

Children often get hurt playing king-of-the-mountain. But the mental hurts can be worse than the cuts, bumps, and breaks that are so common when this game is played. The more you think about it, the more stupid the "king-of-the-mountain" game becomes. Yet every day this game of put-down is played by children, by teens, and even by adults, sometimes by those who are supposed to love each other. How anyone thinks popularity can be won by constantly bumping people off the mountain is difficult to understand.

You may have noticed a group of students who migrate to a school parking lot to smoke. Why does this ritual happen? Why do they smoke in the first place? Why would anyone intentionally smoke when lung cancer, heart disease, and emphysema are such well-known consequences? Everyone knows about them. Yet more people begin to smoke every day, and those who have already begun usually keep doing it, in spite of the risks. The risks are dismissed with the notion that "it won't happen to me." Whenever you see a person taking a big chance, he or she has probably thought "It won't happen to me." But what is the real reason people start smoking? It couldn't be a desire to breathe in smoke. Burning weeds or grass rolled up in paper from one's mouth can't be very appealing. But what does seem appealing is to be like the crowd.

Being accepted by a group seems very important at times, and some people are so anxious to be recognized by someone, anyone, that they will do anything for this acceptance.

But a crowd doesn't think. A crowd often does things with no thought about consequences. Those who don't go along are identified as "chicken." At the slightest hesitation about smoking, drinking beer, stealing something, smoking grass, shooting speed, or whatever, the person is called "chicken." The crowd doesn't stop there. The word *chicken* becomes a chorus, over and over—by individuals and by the group together. The pressure gets tougher and all too often the crowd wins. Sometimes the word *chicken* never has to be said—there is just the implication that it will be said.

Dreading this, many follow the crowd without the first taunt or tease. This is like surrender with no battle.

When we know about this game, or the psychology of a crowd, it's much easier to avoid getting trapped. In fact, it's rather fun to be one-up on the crowd. Sometimes it might be a real honor to be called "chicken." A person strong enough to resist the crowd is certainly no "chicken." In fact, a person tough enough to hold up against the pressure of a crowd is just the opposite from what the group may call "chicken." Doing what's right gives a person a tremendous feeling of accomplishment. Winning a skirmish with a crowd is a real victory. Prisoners-of-war who have suffered much torment pride themselves on withstanding all the efforts of the enemy to make them compromise their principles. Accomplishing this victory automatically admits a person to a very select group. At the moment it may not seem apparent, but somewhere there are superior friends who also pride themselves in doing what's right. Good friends can be found—but how?

That's what Fred had been trying to figure out. He wanted friends more than anything. Dependable and a hard worker, he had a lot going for him. But he had lots against him too, much of which was totally unfair. He was teased and ridiculed all through grade school and junior high school about one thing or another. Often the cutting comments were about something he couldn't do anything about, such as about his worn-out pants—the only pair he had.

When he was teased, Fred snapped back. Every once in a while he tore into one of his tormentors. This got him in trouble at school on several occasions. Once he was so upset that he smashed a chair against a bookcase, and another time he punched a hole in the wall. This went on for years. The vicious cycle kept rolling. Then came high school and more of the same.

Fred had been working at two jobs while going to school, and most of his earnings went to his family. But he had saved enough to make the school prom a big event, including flowers for his date and dinner at a fancy restaurant. But every girl he asked, all five of them, said no. This was a crushing defeat.

More than anything in the world, Fred wanted someone to talk to, someone to go places with, someone to be his friend. He had lots of ability. He knew how to work. He could fix anything. He was kind to the younger neighbor children whom others pushed around. He understood their problems and was a great friend to them. But in his own peer group it was a different story. He always knew no one liked him.

Then something happened. Fred decided to forget about his problems. He forgot about his needs. He forgot about how much he needed friends, and became a friend to everyone around. He became interested in people. He listened to them. He also gave out a few sincere compliments. He even complimented his teachers. This was definitely new. There were no more "put-downs" from him. He still swallowed a few from others, but he pushed himself to think of something good to say about those around him.

Fred also began helping people—everyone, whether they asked or not. He went out of his way to do things for those who had been so cruel to him over the years. About the same time he sharpened up his appearance, which improved the image he had of himself and his needs, and he thought about others. As he started being a friend, he started making friends, and soon he had lots of them.

That's the secret of attracting friends—being a friend. By listening, complimenting, and helping, you can fill people's basic needs. Everyone needs to feel that someone really listens to him and really understands his problems. And when criticisms seem to come from all sides, it's a special treat to be complimented once in a while. Finally, when you can't do something, or don't know how, it's nice to have someone willing to be patient with you and to help you. So learning to listen, compliment, and help is an important part of learning to be a good friend.

Most people are "me" people all through their childhood years. Some never outgrow this; they stay "me" oriented all their lives. Maturity comes and friendships grow when a person stops being a "me" person and discovers that being a friend can be really fun.

The kinds of friends you have now, or will have soon, will probably determine the kind of person you will marry. Are your friends telestial or celestial caliber?

People seem to be attracted to people who are like themselves. Those who drink and smoke are not usually very comfortable around those who talk about missions. Sometimes people think they are going to change later. Sometimes they do, but often they don't. That's why it's important to be on a celestial level right now. How? Live as if you were a celestial-level person. Do all the things you think a celestial person should do. Then your interests will parallel those of other celestial-type people. They will be your closest friends. Why is this important? Because from among your friends, or their friends, will come that special someone whom you will marry. Choosing the right *someone* will make the difference between happiness and sadness. More importantly, happiness with an eternal partner can go on forever if you qualify. It's worth being a good friend, because you will have the same kind of friends that you are—forever.

Is It Really Love?

Is it really love? This doesn't seem like a very difficult question, but the answer isn't always obvious even when things seem clear and the future bright.

Sometimes what seems like love may actually be loving the idea of being in love. It's easy to confuse *wanting* to be in love with really *being* in love. And sometimes one person is in love and the other is not sure. Also, it's possible the match-up is good, but the timing isn't. Time may solve the problem, and then again it might not.

"To every thing there is a season, and a time to every purpose under the heaven: A time to be born, and a time to die; a time to plant, and a time to pluck up that which is planted." (Ecclesiastes 3:1-2.) We might add that there is a time to marry. Hurrying into a wrong choice can be tragic. On the other hand, there might be a time when continually postponing a decision may not be wise either. Knowing what the right timing is may be as important as finding the right person.

Choosing a marriage partner is an interesting example of free agency and consequences. Few decisions are as far-

reaching. When you ponder your possible future with a person, many questions come to mind. "What is important?" "Does this really matter?" "Is this the person I want to share breakfast with each morning—forever?" "What about a joint checking account?" "Will she be a good mother?" "What kind of dad will he be?" "Do I really want her forever?" "Is he really likely to make it—I mean, endure to the end?" You have probably thought about these questions and a thousand others. The answers certainly help answer the big question, "Is it really love?"

The amount of commitment in a relationship is one means of measuring a person's feelings, your own and a friend's as well. Commitment is an essential part of a forever marriage. Promising oneself to someone forever is much more than saying "I do" in a civil ceremony. Commitment means being willing to make things go when they're at their worst. And no matter how wonderful love seems, and how perfect a marriage, there are going to be some bumps. There are going to be some days when there is no more money. Sooner or later the washing machine will quit—if there is a washer. Almost for sure there will be a day now and then with no hot water. There will be hard times, sickness, and likely some heartache. There will be lots of dirty dishes, dirty clothes, and other chores. On occasion the house is going to be a mess. There will be endless demands on time you think should be yours. There will be some moments when you will be left alone. There will be differences of opinion.

At times it may seem as if maybe it's not worth it. But commitment can get a couple past these hurdles—and more. When marriage begins with commitment, you both know that it's going to work even with these many trials and discouragements. Marriage isn't just for the good times and happy days—it's for every day that comes along.

Commitment, which is an even bigger part of love than sex, helps make a marriage a success. Perhaps an important question to ask yourself is, "Am I ready to be unconditionally committed to this person?" When a couple feel that commitment to each other is unconditional, it's time for some serious considerations.

After much careful evaluation, a spiritual confirmation about the question "Is it really love?" can be most comforting. The Lord has told us:

"But, behold, I say unto you, that you must study it out in your mind; then you must ask me if it be right, and if it is right I will cause that your bosom shall burn within you; therefore, you shall feel that it is right.

"But if it be not right you shall have no such feelings, but you shall have a stupor of thought that shall cause you to forget the thing which is wrong." (D&C 9:8-9.)

This process works. Ask all the questions you can. Do all the interviewing possible. Observe what happens under stress and other circumstances. Check out spirituality. Consider other qualifications you think are important. Evaluate what life would be like living together. Think about likes and dislikes. Consider the economics involved, both present and future. Talk to each other about all these things and more. Friends, roommates, and family members may be able to help in many ways. Ask them.

Very likely you shop around quite a bit when you buy something you really want. Getting the best value for your money makes sense. When Melinda said she was on her way to buy a car, everyone expected to see it the next morning. But the next morning Melinda caught a ride as usual—no new car. The same thing happened the next day, and the next. She checked out more cars than an automobile magazine writer. This went on and on. She considered six different kinds of cars quite seriously. She had just about decided on four of them over a period of several weeks. She asked everyone she knew what they thought of this car and that one. She checked capabilities and qualifications. She made intelligent comparisons and finally, months after she had decided to buy her car, she bought it.

Melinda spent more time evaluating cars and choosing one than many people do in choosing a marriage partner. And this was about a car that may last only a few years or may be traded in sooner. Many marriages begin with little attention to making a good choice. Many begin with the attitude that if things don't work out, it doesn't matter much because a change can be made.

If you don't like a new car it can be sold or traded in on another one. Even though many people don't think so, a marriage is totally different.

When you have found someone very special and have considered every factor you think is important, share your conclusions with your Heavenly Father. Talk with him in prayer, telling him everything that is in your heart and mind, and ask him if your decision is right. Then patiently be in tune for an answer. Listen, and if it is right he will cause that your bosom will burn within you; therefore, you will feel that it is right.

Marriage is just a beginning. There will be some holes in socks and some gloomy moments. But the many happy moments can be more wonderful than words can describe. Together you can build your own quiet world, in life and in eternity. Sharing life together with someone you love is what life and the gospel and eternity are all about.

The Lord has given us this counsel:

"And again, verily I say unto you, if a man marry a wife by my word, which is my law, and by the new and everlasting covenant, and it is sealed unto them by the

Holy Spirit of promise, by him who is anointed, unto whom I have appointed this power and the keys of this priesthood; and it shall be said unto them—Ye shall come forth in the first resurrection; and if it be after the first resurrection, in the next resurrection; and shall inherit thrones, kingdoms, principalities, and powers, dominions, all heights and depths—then shall it be written in the Lamb's Book of Life, that he shall commit no murder whereby to shed innocent blood, and if ye abide in my covenant, and commit no murder whereby to shed innocent blood, it shall be done unto them in all things whatsoever my servant hath put upon them, in time, and through all eternity; and shall be of full force when they are out of the world; and they shall pass by the angels, and the gods, which are set there, to their exaltation and glory in all things, as hath been sealed upon their heads, which glory shall be a fulness and a continuation of the seeds forever and ever.

"Then shall they be gods, because they have no end; therefore shall they be from everlasting to everlasting, because they continue; then shall they be above all, because all things are subject unto them. Then shall they be gods, because they have all power, and the angels are subject unto them." (D&C 132:19-20.)

You can have all of these blessings, if you always remember who you are. You can have the best in this life and in eternity: a choice companion, children, and an eternal family. And you will know it's really love.